SAY SAND

SAY SAND

DANIEL COUDRIET

CARNEGIE MELLON UNIVERSITY PRESS
PITTSBURGH 2010

ACKNOWLEDGMENTS

Grateful acknowledgment is made to the editors of journals where several of these poems have previously appeared, often in different versions:

American Letters & Commentary: "Replacing the Question About Babies," "Merienda," "Wheat"
Blackbird: "Necessary Authorities"
The Cincinnati Review: "Rosario, Funes, Roldán"
Conjunctions: "Primary Education," "Because It Had Always Been a Quiet Town," "In Another Life the Stones"
Crazyhorse: "Grief," "Interior View"
Denver Quarterly: "What It Will Be Like In Bouquets," "How Far That Sound," "I Couldn't Find a Forest"
Front Porch: "Fair Warning," "My Throat Swallowing Makes the Sound Daughter"
Fulcrum: "I Had To Write Exile," "I'm Measuring Myself the Distance From Her"
Good Foot: "Onions"
Harvard Review: "Reservations"
Indiana Review: "The Rodents"
The Iowa Review: "There Is More Ocean Around Us"
Mississippi Review: "Proem (as "Geese")
New Orleans Review: "Romance Language," "Romance Language," "Romance Language"
Octopus Magazine: "Lyric," "Sonnet," "The Dinner Party"
Parthenon West Review: "Naming the City"
Stride (U.K.): "Privacy," "None Of Them Would Stop," "All That I Wanted"
Swink: "Without Reservations"
Verse: "The Detectives," "Schemers," "Alibi," "The Bouzouki Falling Into Itself an Endless," "Bright Size Life," "The Tunnel"

Grateful acknowledgment is also made to the editors of *Best American Fantasy* (Prime Books, 2007) for selecting the poem "Geese" to be anthologized among their pages. "Geese" appears in this manuscript as the untitled *Proem*.

Book design: M. Callen, Kyle Rood

The publication of this book is made possible by a grant from the Pennsylvania Council on the Arts.

Library of Congress Control Number 2009930162
ISBN 978-0-88748-518-3
Copyright © 2010 by Daniel Coudriet
All rights reserved
Printed and bound in the United States of America

10 9 8 7 6 5 4 3 2 1

para Mariela
y
para Joaquín

CONTENTS

Proem   11

I
THE BOUZOUKI FALLING INTO ITSELF AN ENDLESS   15
THE DETECTIVES   16
RESERVATIONS   17
INTERIOR VIEW   18
NECESSARY AUTHORITIES   19
PRIVACY   20
BODY AS ELEGY   21
ROMANCE LANGUAGE   23
BRIGHT SIZE LIFE   24

II
LYRIC   33
ALL THAT I WANTED   35
GRIEF   36
WHAT IT WILL BE LIKE IN BOUQUETS   37
THE TUNNEL   38
WITHOUT RESERVATIONS   40
PRIMARY EDUCATION   41
NAMING THE CITY   42
THE RODENTS   43
SONNET   44
THERE IS MORE OCEAN AROUND US   45
HOTEL NOCHE   46
HOW FAR THAT SOUND   47

III

I HAD TO WRITE EXILE   51

CHARRED BELOVED   54

ROSARIO, FUNES, ROLDÁN   55

CHARRED BELOVED   56

MERIENDA   57

CHARRED BELOVED   58

THE DINNER PARTY   59

CHARRED BELOVED   64

REPLACING THE QUESTION ABOUT BABIES   65

CHARRED BELOVED   66

IV

I'M MEASURING MYSELF THE DISTANCE FROM HER   69

ROMANCE LANGUAGE   70

BECAUSE IT HAD ALWAYS BEEN A QUIET TOWN   71

FAIR WARNING   72

RECIPE   73

MY THROAT SWALLOWING MAKES THE SOUND DAUGHTER   74

SCHEMERS   75

I COULDN'T FIND A FOREST   77

WHEAT   78

ALIBI   79

ONIONS   80

ROMANCE LANGUAGE   81

IN ANOTHER LIFE THE STONES   82

UNCOMFORTABLE THE ROADSIDE DUST WE SPEAK   83

NONE OF THEM WOULD STOP   84

SAY SAND

The geese in the pond took me from my stroller, their horrible bills pinching and mangling my flabby toddler arms, my soft belly. I kicked them like hollow watermelons when they snapped at my genitals.

The woman in the paddleboat with her two little girls. The smallest one's head turned to a balloon, sprouted a string (which her tiny fingers slid quickly around) and she floated away.

"You're too young to be worried about a family," the woman said. I could feel pondwater soaking through my overalls. She tried to load me into her boat. "This water we can use to grow more skin, to make a new sister," she said to her one little girl, watching her old sister float.

"I didn't get to attach a note to her with our address," the girl pouted, "in case she gets found."

"She no longer has all of her parts," the woman said.

Another woman spreading bread crusts into the edge of the water. Her family is laying a path of stones out into the pond, leaping from one stone to the next. I want her to be mother.

I raise my arms, but the geese have taken them. I raise my legs, but my skin has already drained out of my pants with the pondwater. I cannot find my genitals without the geese, honking all around me, and because there is language spilled everywhere, I am touching nothing.

I

THE BOUZOUKI FALLING INTO ITSELF AN ENDLESS

And after the starlings have squawked away
the architecture is obvious—the air with its fish
full of sand. This river too wide to build.

Here is night, its cloak lined with thorns
where girls in shawls with bioluminescent bellies
look for the wires we all know hold the puppets.
Whichever of us the puppets.

And all of us speaking at the same time
of marriage & the green of her mother's mirror.
Of boxes & screens, the plants we've carted
across town & screens, the cardboard apparatus

where someone has written "by collecting
what you are not" or "to fall is to surrender
the shape of your body" & we are trying to read
comparing the shapes of our bodies

to the wind as it rushes over the field of eggs.
Clouds like trailed undergarments,
the forest floor covered with splintered axe handles,
the moon a throat filled by a swallowed tongue.

THE DETECTIVES

They are holding a picture of the lost,
Sammy. The dog wearing a bathrobe.
And I'm on the lawn, across the street
from the flagpole that Charles speaks to,
wearing my bathrobe—red terry-cloth pelt
cut from a red terry-cloth beast. My robe
that matches Sammy's, my brethren in pelt,
although I've never seen him. Honestly,
I am not sure that I am not the dog.
The detectives are beautiful women,
they ask the questions. One of them, from France
with hair like tying red strings to bees
and painting the patterns. It's so funny
to see her in her coat, the one she was wearing
yesterday, with an enormous magnifying glass,
looking around. Her sneakers are new
and she photographs all the fire hydrants.
And the other, the South American,
is the woman I long to drive on sidewalks with,
to collect her from her house full of sweets,
to embroider designs on the legs of her jeans.
It is raining, her glasses are broken,
the frame cracked in the middle. Charles shouts
that the space program's interest in Mars
has caused the change in weather patterns,
and we are all listening. Though we worry more
about Sammy, the dog we cannot find.

RESERVATIONS

The podium with the women in black,
the bracelet they are holding toward us,
whose fingernail clippings is it made of,
whose small enough ribs? Lost as I am

this body, the sleeves I hold up,
the strands of canaries that hop out.
Clinking down the bar. Clinking of

her fingernails, arabesques of beetles
crossing the tablecloth. Speak to them,
they will not roll up into shells of butter.

They will not become small hampers
of bread. They will not wear bread.
These fingers of bread.

INTERIOR VIEW

Their devices for holding horses together
lining the walls in neat rows, as if a splinter might burst
at any moment, a rain of hooves on the bamboo roof
that keeps the barrels cold & the same
as they slowly absorb & flavor what they are holding
& hold gradually less. This probable life
of a cooper as each slat is carefully bent
or the rings are hammered around more of them,
the grapes not sharing any affections
in the troughs with odd-shaped bottles suckling
the edges. And if we inverse a cow,
stretch the skin neatly over a log frame,
if we crush the entire harvest against its skin,
there are caves running under the mountains
where atmosphere is shadows in chunks of ice,
deep blue with shadows & channels of white.
This is where we bury the clouds.

NECESSARY AUTHORITIES

What stone is telling this story, the silences
of a palm pressed into a steering wheel,
slowing for the guardhouse where they hunt
for flies smuggled in the fruit.

Signs warning of wandering animals,
of notifying the piles of green parrots
dead by the road, the turkey vultures
not far off.
      The no narrative of endless grasses
and islands of trees—
a horse standing ankle-deep in the flood,
its bridle neatly attached to a signpost.

Not even the mice we feel climbing our necks
as we sleep can tell us of the infidelities,
the way we costume our own hands
or a clear lake means there are two skies.

PRIVACY

The bus with its interior cut from scraps
of sweaters a team of grandmothers
has been knitting—the grandmothers
of former lovers.

Trying to convince these children
that the chickens are moving
according to wireless remote controls
held by men more handsome

than imagined jaguars, the bloated ones
that are chewing my torso. Always
the men hanging at the corners
comfortably in the blue nooses they wear.

But who is the one pushing that cart
containing all of the fingers
that have touched me intimately?
The matches I swallowed, striking now
off my ribs, tiny warmths like caterpillars.

BODY AS ELEGY

The sorrow of a horse is coming
from the awkward postures of lovemaking

& the word begat has no belonging here,
moth wings. Paper cuts collecting

in my gut each time I inhale.
Forgive me if I cannot return the music

in my head sounds good enough
cries of babies, I'm greedy for knowing why.

On my birth, I come in from hiding
in sounds I've been meaning to speak

to you about your eyes of late hours
& their unlikely skill for rubbings of headstones.

Floral life of my throat.
Circular walls, silent & banished

from the theater, everything arcing away.
What should we call these creatures,

flowers?
My arrivals with wax replicas of hands

& the others we need
we need water.

My brain plans to fear my body,
no place for a fire

its guests no longer speak of beginnings.
Of me,

youngish prolonged intimacies.
I could not lie could not sleep

could not suffer.
Broken off arm, offering

to the others, waiting at the docks
when everyone else is asleep.

I'll tell you in my plainest voice
hers is what I must.

ROMANCE LANGUAGE

Language the product of absence. How seldom
we summon the janitors for our emergencies
anymore. Sawdust spilling from the jars

in the closet, unmarked crates full of absinthe
have replaced our deck furniture. This effort
to disremember my tongue,
                                 strewn scene
of bongos and ex-cigars, flags and the small fires
outside encampments.
                                      César bursting
through the door with a plunger.
                                      The cries were erotic.

BRIGHT SIZE LIFE

There are two languages for father,
                                  my almost watching water
and it displaced by a body of my father's skin
                                                    when he was born.

My father's body is in a clear plastic box with tubes, attached
to my arms, the yellow of his skin is him trying to become
my fragments.
                My arm, digging,
                                      I used to borrow
archaeology somewhere making mountains into ash.

I cannot describe the somewhere of skin
the way water is not above, but inside ash.

I am not mailing ashes to anyone. The plastic box, tubes, the bags
                    with liquid, watching them fill with ashes
that I am not mailing as language.

And my arms are rarely inside hands. How a touch is apart
or requesting something into the skin.

                        How these ribs are beautiful
and have nearly made myself this room.

                                                          What we watch for
sliding beneath skin or water or the voice of this air shaking inside us
is language.
                                      As the road bright yellow and the car is stopping
and surrounding myself with sounds of my father listening.

I am talking again about concrete, and the dream of us not being

and the roads, when a dotted line, light, sound that girls skip down, holding hands and coats, when a dotted line and swinging, upwards, feet in the air and chains.

                                        So drawing lines,
so there is a shape of body that is a line, a shape of boy that is a line
and muted colors I cannot tell.

                        The sand, and the sand
moving. When there is gravel pushed into piles,
my collection of rocks without names.

And there are more birds here than not,
                                I cannot speak body
or skin and have it mean anything other
            than plastic boxes have held everyone, language,
                                    my father's body,
cradled in water.

And there is a square without flowers, without girls skipping down,

                        something about the unspoken string
of road at night, headlights and the trees are painted white, the fields vacant and no light, and headlights on the trees,
                                            painted white,
body that I touched.

The wind is trying to hold the birds that we toss.

II

LYRIC

Night, blue field of snow
like a room
a sidewalk through the middle,
plowed, field mice
skating there.

And I look up from my frying pan
full of ice cubes,
another in a series of love letters
to my therapist,
who reminds me to be sad.

And the flapjacks I'm making
will be sad and malformed.

Silhouette of a stroller being pulled
by wolves,
the baby inside blue

but alive, with eyes like ashtrays.
I bring it home to you,
not my therapist,

and we set the basket on the stove
to thaw. It goes up in flames,

but the baby's still
blue, blue as before.
It runs out into the night

using ping pong paddles as snowshoes—
odd footprints like graves
for my flapjacks.

ALL THAT I WANTED

Philosophers, how many teeth have you bent
on the needles that are subways
splaying voices the way coral sounds

to the fish swimming there?
                 My arm movements are saliva
collecting at the corners of mouths,
the several I've brought with me
from home.
                I can never find enough
clay in the soil. How little I can make
with my hands.
                        Don't ever begin
it by asking.
                           Unsafe feet,
red pencils and candlesticks, all that I wanted
was to create a room in which to be loved.

GRIEF

The way the stone builds itself,
the stone containing a wound made of air.

In a field, the ones tossing my teardrops
& the ones filling bodies with stones,
enclosing the stones. My body longing

to be made of air. Everything is held
to enclose things around a tear & is

quietly crying. The young girls with arms
of daisies, one girl with beautiful lips,
her mouth. To enclose her,

the wound is still.

WHAT IT WILL BE LIKE IN BOUQUETS

Unbothered by traffic of houseguests,
a childhood before the city's windows
of pastries & the element is heating up—
our children rolling past the stove door

& when will they walk is all anyone asks
while I've seen three cats bound over
the concrete wall & lick the sleeping faces.

There is no way to walk you through
this room, smoke, before the attic door swings
open to its rotted stairway, its sharpeners
at each corner. Can we make a life,

mosquitoes nesting in our bath towels
waiting for the pastries to come, neatly,
in little paper bags with ribbons.

THE TUNNEL

The fields you set on fire
over a face that wouldn't leave

the stalks, the self reborn
in stacks of ash. Spider banjo

when I tiptoed on cobblestones
with her small small feet

I thought a harp might chase
us into the studios, I thought

glass might make a window
always appear in front of us

and that flowers might burn
and carpet our path. Guitar

of your lap, I am sliding on you,
please try not to sound sad.

I resent finding myself in a cemetery,
digging a tunnel.

The rain is red corridors of mascara
leaking her eyes. It will be a piano

creeping up behind us that makes us
say banjo makes us hold our tongues

and fresco the lampshades, natal
glow of walls, doorframes, hallways.

Clouds of feathers are emerging
from the flutes that you keep hidden.

The breeze, an incision
the way I build my mouth

like a stairwell,
syrup on the kitchen floor.

That is years after the bar closed
in on us. The tunnel we found,

as if we'd recognized each other
in the ashes puffing down the streets,

both only wanting to ask if the fire
had happened. I'm with the fish

beneath you. In mirrors
there are more voices.

The piano, descending
like imprints of feet on stone or lips,

the sun which is blue and what
will no longer grow in two hands,

the children she left there
as we move scythe-like into the field.

WITHOUT RESERVATIONS

We supposed they were forming families,
the lights moving into the dark glasses

the knuckle I find floating in my soup
splits my lip. I am reaching with fingers

I no longer control. The ring I brushed
off her red lips, blue stone of her mouth.

The sky is a mouth.
Blue stone of her mouth.

And the women in black showing us our seats.
And the women are floating papers above candles

on tiny filaments of wire. When I swallow
the roof is peeled back out of view

and we pile up small houses for birds.
And the women are floating off balconies

buoyed upward by their breasts. I reach
them with fingers that may not be mine.

PRIMARY EDUCATION

All of the children held in a blue sweater,
who is it knitting them together with tiny thumbs.

The tiny hoods they must wear as they blanket
the corn exploding in its refusal to warm,
the tiles of the sidewalk as uncorrected teeth
in a kettle.
                      The light switches painted
red with fingernail polish. The slats of wood
they've used to cover the windows.

Somewhere in a room, the well-dressed
are talking & naming a country after a girl.

Somewhere without a name the ice is falling
as it melts & all of the people in the streets
have never seen snow—its exhalation—

NAMING THE CITY

The story of fire is my mother's spleen,
half of it a stone in a child's bathing suit
spreading out around a body, the salt.

And bending over the sidewalk is lying down
on a cement block, without garden, & praying
an officer will notice there is no boiler in the alley,
no excuse for leaving the tent, for renaming the rain
a window, a hand held there.

        The trunk at the base of the bed
with letters from your daughter,

                the one that hasn't been born,
is a speck that hasn't blossomed into stone
into blood on a sidewalk. The steps you take,

the circumference of my mother, suspended there
above the river.

THE RODENTS

Whether they crawl out of the ground, shaven,
disguising themselves as potatoes. Or they are hiding
themselves now beside my fingers—two sleeping litters
of bones. Apnea curls up in the mouth of a sleepless toddler,
still contemplating the late hours of his father
not returning. Not a furry mass, disembodied beard
skirting the darkened rooms, the upstairs hallway,
light that burns into the night. Flocking to our house,
they offer themselves as an ivy of pink flesh, piling
over the windows, sucking air like warm leaves.

SONNET

You cannot understand my sadness,
my stomach a dripping rag
on a post at the end of our herb garden.

A pack of chihuahuas, each of them missing
front legs from the wheelbarrow accident,
yapping and hopping like shrunken kangaroos.

My heart on a string. That someone
using it like a yo-yo, the splatter paint
of blood all down the sidewalk.

It's on the glasses of the little girl
sucking her thumb. It's on the tongues
outstretched of the chihuahuas

who are always following mindlessly,
the heart lowering, raising.

THERE IS MORE OCEAN AROUND US

Being inside a harpsichord is the jewelry box that I am inside.

The hand inside my hand is the all-night fortune teller's hand.
Small puppies sleep at our ankles.

I am with the fleas, gathering about the eyelashes
with their tiny flip flops.

HOTEL NOCHE

The cold white of kitchens with pincushions
we're attached our names. The shirts they've given us
to wear dangle us our bodies. If the window is large enough,
if a hallway is built & the room filling with guitar.

Of yellow bonnet clutter, plinking piano keys
with signs the spaces. Walking home predawn
the blues is this:
                    behind us, the doors sliding shut
& the distance. We're busy reinforcing the walls,

& I'm carrying my brother, I'm carrying
huge planks of driftwood we've removed,
the always slope of the yard from the fence
of yardsticks, the overturned cups the strings

by our arms. There is nothing of hotel rooms,
outside everywhere people wander the hallways.

HOW FAR THAT SOUND

The cabinets of files written on little cards

& the mother leading her child down the hallway,
a school or hospital,
        or the child alone looking
out the bus window at the grasses' one expression
      & either child crying—

& the sun in this town means more snow is falling
over the Andes,
        forgetting itself & blurring
the tops of the mountains
        like ink spreading into skin.

And maybe there is a city where all of the babies
      that were thoughts or almost are abandoned

& speaking them makes them now but our hands
never reach them in these vines, all of them now
brown & dry & cracked.
        The wires hissing
between the poles & always the birds

      like the birds disappearing
into their nests of mud. The barrels of olives
      lined up outside the windows
& the several mouths drinking from this river.

III

I HAD TO WRITE EXILE

Allow the ones of them not in front of you,
those in skinny heels and evening gowns as they totter,
to bring bottles of wine from the bodegas,

watch them wander the enormous steel containers,
the city of fermentation, or imagine wrists and bracelets
over the shopping basket, and now watching them

sit on the side of your mattress with the corkscrew
already twisted. And it is not the proper climate
for an exiled Russian magician, whether he can die or not

is immaterial to which of them has used eyeliner,
which of them is not her self but is water freezing
just as you open the tap, is marbles colliding

with flesh and a smell of gunpowder, cannonballs
and a field too wide to see its ending, is steam
from the grates, the bodegas. Federico,

too much of you in front of this stucco door,
combing your hair in a reflection, the sun
and these forty-three sailors, the sun on your skin

coming at you from deep in a corridor—or outside
the shadows are eyeliners—and echoes of boots
coming in the corridor, knocking the doorway,

Federico, these are the men that will shoot you
with the moon and a smell of gunpowder, the yard
too wide to see its ending. For one of them, the clock

is approaching, is above the street he is walking,
for one of them it is morning, the depth of red
we are reaching into, it reaching into fabric and sand

and night. And there are staccato brushstrokes, violets,
with clusters, petals of white, sails as boats or gondolas
in the ravines the arroyos below the footbridges

and her in her white dress, night and the petals, ribbons
the breeze I had to write this poem until the hotel's sign
red, neon, and extinguishing gradually itself outward

and the field of undergrowth reaches out from stucco
and all of the crickets breathing the ground, the way
hair and tension and a string and tension vibrate

the interior of the wood. And all of the crickets
moving above the soil I had to write soil, with air down
between it, all of them their legs down between it

and moving down into it and some of the beetles
wriggle and squirm. All of them with shells, red, neon
and the reflections, horizons, small gravitations

over fields of vineyards getting smaller and smaller,
the bodega outside Maipú, and hands over the wood slats,
the wagon between the ruts, the museum of wagons

and rough hands and the leaves the grapes between fingertips.
The green knives as they flash and fill baskets, the grapes
on the bottoms, the weight, and bits of liquid escaping

to the soil. The green knives as they flash and retreat,
the rhythm of the wheels moving over the ruts
and the lanterns hanging across streets, he is walking

the baskets resting on the sidewalks, the night's voices
behind shutters, the forty-three sailors singing like vibrations
and ribbons of lights over streets. The ribbons trailing

from her white dress as she is rounding the corner always
a step away, the puddles her eyeliner, her reflections
approaching from the windows, rough hands against

windows, corridors from eyes, heat, the moon is not what
I had to write her reflection, the red fabric sliding off skin
extinguishing between fingertips, the tension, vibration.

CHARRED BELOVED

Arshile
carrying your daughter
around your neck,
starving

your mother outside
the door of your shed
with each step
the colors washing away
from your shapes.

                You vomit

shed wood canvas color,
but there is no landscape,
no country
of your liver.

No banners, no aprons
beside the stew.

No seeing her dark eyes
that city between rivers
the sky reaches for you
liquid ink paint night.

Her dark eyes
before her screams—

and your daughter born,
screaming
the world.

ROSARIO, FUNES, ROLDÁN

The rim of hubcaps, the dogs yelping and brake lights
the inflation of air in my ear, on edges, the rim of hubcaps
dented and pressed. A steeple, flat roofs and occasional bricks,
curtains, a window just ajar, her handprint. Around her
the autos coming, the intersection from all four directions,
and brake lights, inflation and flow, his arm around her
crossing the street the old men the chairs and the sidewalk
the café the old men speaking occasional hum and hiccup
the tree branches rubbing the roof of the bus, splinters.
Occasional drift of taxis, the radio speaking its splinters
the yelp and brake lights, the couple riding and learning
with a whisper there is a baby coming, crossing the street
to the needle her arm the inflation, occasional drift, hum
in my ear. The curtain and his wife behind it with another man
examining her, how will they divide the autos into lanes,
motorbikes flowing in and out, not hearing her handprint.

CHARRED BELOVED

Mother,
the river is flowing
over everything I touch.

Arshile
carrying the stew
on your skin it is
burning you
with people
you follow
at night.

MERIENDA

All of them I'm writing by looking with their silver trays
of croissants spilling, polished black shoes shuffling by.
I'm writing you the wires our voices will be hovering
around in the sand, we say sand to mean buried
and I've kept recordings of the voices of relatives.

I will know my nationality by what frightens me
and my inability to properly speak the names
they keep passing to me. "Please give me your image,
my fluency, by looking half a block down the street,
the bright white building of their wedding, the five buses
we switch as we travel to the mouth."

Our driver with the name of my nephew and a cracked windshield,
what can the cigar smell from his lunch or the streamers
on his mirrors bring us of the puppies on the roof
next door, the man inside trying to hang himself?

"Don't write angel," he is saying from the rafters,
"don't write the children too large for me to travel."
"I've already come for them with coffee and croissants,"
says his wife. "Why do you keep losing me in your sleep?"

CHARRED BELOVED

                Waiting,
your daughter
exploring the leaves,
the thickets,
and shouting to you—

how would it sound
the boots crushing
your liver inside you—

no, crushing the leaves,
cracked veins
bloodroot bootprints.

She is drawing pictures
on the floor.

Who is keeping those fish
from freezing, the ones deep
in the rivers?

                Whose hands
are these pulling my skin
into shapes we are eating?

THE DINNER PARTY

The mice are surprising hosts.
All of them circulate upon each other like a scampering rug.

Legs of the woman, uncertain of their intentions, her floral dress
and her calves frozen like stumps

and we all feel sorry as the mice scurry over her
the way small animals creep through the snow.

The room as a sneeze, in a crowd, all clotted.

We cringe as they climb the white nylon.

The mice with tiny gloves on their paws in the courtyard.

She shrieking in French, unmentionables,
they leave little prints, at night, aware they might freeze.

It is astonishing.

To imagine how they maintain the gardens and all of the flowers are painted fingertips.

And adorning vases all over the house.

My wrist, they've eaten it. And they've left me elaborate equations on the dining room walls.

Sitting in their places, name tags in front of them.

To envision the furry swarm digging and planting.

All of them grown in proportion to the mice, fresh-cut.

As I am thinking, they are nibbling at my hand,
with a pointed brush of a forearm. I use it to paint
a mathematical design.

To explain:
all of the guests written in an indecipherable script
at place settings so small they can scarcely be touched.

Without being crushed.

With the entrée in a covered metal serving tray.

They pull back the cover in a cloud of steam
appearing like a straight line.

China and wine glasses to pick up the utensils:

and here come the mice, the guests tying their minuscule napkins.

It is my severed hand, holding an apple.

CHARRED BELOVED

Arshile
carrying your mother
around your neck,
your daughter
running
her fingers into the ground
until they bleed
into your bootprints,
bootprints,
your mother's apron.

*

A village of newborns
in the apron
rocking to sleep, newborns
rolling in the grass
into thickets
bootprints
leaves
the fire
inside you.

Mother,
you evaporated
into the stew and

shapes cannot carry my colors.

REPLACING THE QUESTION ABOUT BABIES

There is a funnel we are running through barrels,
through charcoal to make certain we can name it "funnel."
There are ants with vast ceilings, buttressing columns, rose windows
in their insteps. A belfry crushing my face with its footprints.

Something is filtering the rows of them walking where the horizon
becomes film, still the ones above us spitting from their windows,
emptying their flower boxes. The soil, discarded funnels, huddling
beneath overhangs, the ants rolling from the impacts.

No language is small enough to name their bones,
                              to keep the poem from emptying
itself everywhere. The broken kitchen appliances have landed
in gutted houses, in washbasins for the babies.

The first of them with giant gloves reaches the funnel
submerged and melts upon touching it. When we open his skull
we find undergarments hidden in the backs of desks,
so many that there weren't any words left.

There is a child kicking around the clearing, a baby with its feet bound
in film. Its insteps are like exhaled legs in the dirt.

Something is digging into the soil, hitting bottom and stopping
realizing flower box and still the ants are climbing through slats.
When it rains, when it rains the word downspout, our hands
have no gloves, which of us are the ones spitting?

Which of us tempted by the coils of copper wiring? We cannot name
ourselves walls. I cannot understand the language of ankles,
whenever I am speaking my lips, my lips make "funnel."

CHARRED BELOVED

Mother,
bootprints
in my vomit
and that man painting
naked
contorted bodies
over my wife's skin,

          painting night
her dark eyes
dancing
the colors away
from your shapes
her shape
in the people
I am

following,
that city charred,
beloved
cracked veins
inside me.

My liver
the door
to my shed.

My daughter is screaming.

IV

I'M MEASURING MYSELF THE DISTANCE FROM HER

How many times I cannot pronounce the piano
making the sound of rain or an ice cube sprouting
felt in my throat as I try to speak the small insects
spiraling in the spotlight & the shadows
of the support holding the grand piano open.
Really, this is about the quivering, the felt,
& whether a string section is playing as I maneuver
the parquet floor towards the trellis by the door
or her reaching my arm & tugging me towards her.
I'm measuring myself the distance from her
& here to the airport, the distance home
from the painted signs indicating a harvest years ago,
the screened porch overlooking a train I cannot
see, & somewhere a stream beneath the roads
& a small metal box inside with linoleum,
a man crouched there looking for ice
by the shadow it makes. In the next town
there is an apartment identical to mine
& I have driven to a large room of people
around a piano sometimes & the wrappers
& shells they leave on the floors after. The planes
pass over so frequently we forget. Some of them
are children with green masks walking up & down
the wooden steps, too many of them with small nibbles
out of the edges. When we hammer the pegs into place
all of our work has been hidden, there is a stage
with lights dimming but neither of us can find a curtain.

ROMANCE LANGUAGE

The spaces in my back are sore from painting the stars
on the ceiling.
                    How many flowers I have smuggled
out of the hospitals.

                    I've become disinterested in bathing.
My body is crowded and smoky
and the water leaves rings that adopt unusual suctions
giving nipples to my toes.

                    Where will we walk
when our footsteps arouse sidewalks?
Some of the desirable water has flooded our balconies.
And the voices are not ours.

BECAUSE IT HAD ALWAYS BEEN A QUIET TOWN

The roof off, letting its bright red hair down as if a sudden fire, as if a nightgown erupting into flames. Nightgowns discarded all over town, noisily leaving puddles of bricks from the foundation. The young boys being seen in their pajamas. The tree until, in a shudder, a legion of green moths. And many tried to help the boy. There was the stout man who was convinced he'd spend all day out there with trashbags to keep things flowing. The tree was really part of his capillary system, full of blood and a bicycle pump, trying. There was the plain little girl whose family donut shop satisfied its sales at the base of the tree to keep him company. She'd bring her dolls and set up a tea party. She imagined that they'd get married. The apartment of the local beauty and her collection of exotic nightgowns grew long and tangled. The firemen didn't have ladders long enough and they used the longer ladders to climb the one renowned for her kindness to firemen. And the boy ate his clothes, his hair, cutting it, then braiding it into various hats hideously long, and he'd break them off, his fingernails grew into utensils, eventually, and broken fingernails.

FAIR WARNING

The carousel operator in backlight, my tuxedo with strings
in the hems, the strings holding her dress.

What the floor blinks I think crosswalk footsteps with sequins.

The inside of my ear angles up, look at the accordion music
seeping out of it, the stains of voices on her legs.

It is the generator hum pumping the distance home
out over the field, someone hammering rust.

We do not live in a parachute.

RECIPE

A sausage is being eaten
quickly at both ends.

When I speak of pebbles
I do not mean teeth.

Dear water, your teeth
are the bracelet
around my neck.

Pebbles are really teeth.

MY THROAT SWALLOWING MAKES THE SOUND DAUGHTER

These clearings where the neighbors build bonfires,
& the mandolin's hot puddles in the backs of my eyes.

We are waiting to enter one of two doors.
I rarely see hair that reminds me of home.

When I meet a rocking chair, I destroy it,
before I add pieces to the fire I dig into the floorboards.

There is a tooth coming in an envelope.
A little girl can be grown with angular water.

SCHEMERS

The feathers I'm plucking from my back
are no longer ideas. All of the chickens

in our town now totally naked, liberated
from their coops. And our huge sack

of feathers and rented Santa suits
providing little but memories of the episodes

that shaped our muscles, hideous gummings
by the victims of organized extractions

of teeth. How serial the maps we had drawn
on our plaid pants, the filing cabinets

that we filled with vast catalogs of teeth.
The only time I remember crying

was when the authorities tossed our evidence
from the upper stories—clattering of the drawers

and the almost liquid spreading of teeth
all over the street. I'd never seen a sky

below us or pulsing lights so intense.
And you might imagine our plan to melt

the enamel into a mold for one giant tooth,
to teach children proper hygiene by visiting

the schools, you might think us to be sadistic
or noble. You might be able to explain

how I am driving on this long road, my bus
filled with the torsos of mannequins

that lean onto each other in horribly romantic
postures, how the feathers are already postmarked

to our families, how the headlights never stop
swimming towards us.

I COULDN'T FIND A FOREST

Where they are sleeping, the citylight dissolving upward outward and how much the city reaches while we wait for its rivers, its scarves glimmering like scales beneath water, like underdeveloped film.

And your thin shins wandering its streets absorbing light, I've seen these fire escapes in a movie backlot, the orchestra, where they are sleeping.

Our heroine, as we join her midway with too much eyeliner, and all the bars letting out, trees skulking over streets, hanging, the low lull of docking, of shore leave, and into and out of the late night theaters, arms, hands, groping, too many scenarios of expectation.

No matter how long we speak, we cannot list unforgettable names, catalog their fears. Where our parents ate breakfast when they didn't know morning.

WHEAT

The machine with thousands of tiny gears mouths for itself.

It is saying everything we miss eating steak.

And that machine has taken another cow, with its mouths
like burning milk.

Even the moon is hot, made of ice and written our names on them.

We learn to read the etchings with our tongues.

ALIBI

To pull the wings off the smoke
the aching the shape of a lily
I am teaching myself to swallow.
When the window is open

I cannot see a reflection in red
my father cannot see red at all
or the lights strung around the borders
of the place where small girls sleep.

The spaces between houses
are not large enough to keep out
the horses that are waiting
for amateur westerns to begin.

No longer mentioning breath
my body is unconcerned with the passage
of conspirators that do not leave marks.
The woman I pass in the street has eaten

severely my mouth the crater in my face
recalls her tenderness. Recalls how my foot
grew its own mouth devoured my mattress
and led me out into the night air

hobbling on its tiny legs and dragging me
behind in the fashion of old firehoses
the ones long enough to reach from the station
to the fire without being carried on a truck.

ONIONS

Knife that I'm holding in my hand,
one hand palm up on the table,
the other wavering inches above.

And onions littering the floor of this room,
the floor's imagined gravity, pulling everything
inward, beneath the weight of the onions.

I've been peeling onions for five months.
My house is filled with them, and with insects
that will outlive me. With skin translucent

like wings of moths, or like ghosts, the onions
are closing off the windows, blocking the light.
They are angels of salt.

ROMANCE LANGUAGE

A truck with strange tubing attached to our ventilation
vacuuming. It is harder to speak.

It says Recycling Center, but we know about the weddings.

I have forgotten what the pronouns mean.
There was a dinner. A long table with families,
but I never recognize who I'm there with.

I cannot blame you.

The angriest divorcées are climbing the fences waving baguettes
like batons with glittery streamers.

IN ANOTHER LIFE THE STONES

Garment bag that I am being stuffed with fur.
Trash bag that I cover myself with against rain.
Air that cannot get inside me, fur already inside me.

The lungs make sedated pets. See them resting,
the girls' laps like tired kittens
or like scalps. See them hugging the fur
to their faces. The kitten I named

the sound of sausages sizzling in a pan.
How it streaks the house, the walls, the furniture
as it greases by. How it scalds my hands
even as I reach for it. It cannot hurt the girls,

faces blank and pale and night. Their breathing
is what makes the fur breathe. Their scent
is what wanders us into the yard next door,

the garage with no door and its barking dogs.
The location of night and the rattling of sticks
against the walls, scratching of paws
and the sizes we imagine for those dogs
behind stone walls. Girl fingers rubbing stone.

In another life the stones left by ploughs.
These stones that are bruises.
These stones are heads for dolls.

UNCOMFORTABLE THE ROADSIDE DUST WE SPEAK

There is no gazebo measuring itself the hillside
& the children rolling down. I'm losing them,
the vowels slipping out of my jaw make me obvious

as traveler. Obvious the hay we're making by not watering,
the not here of security rummaging my bag at each stack
of books their ladders seem inappropriate. Flower boxes,

phone lines reconcile the balconies & not rubber
trees but trees made of rubber. What noises
the breeze the ditches bringing water down mountains

make me obvious as unwatered, city, how you leave me
as I walk through you carrying her tired body. No story
of blond hair asleep or fountains spurting tiny globes of glass,

strands of wires—which ones of them the lightbulbs
bubbling over each other in the ditches & not breaking.

NONE OF THEM WOULD STOP

Laughing, the sudden taxidermies
leaving the field a mixture
of recent animals, inanimates,
and I'd raise laughers there,
if I could locate them, each in a cherry
picker, and the children would walk
through with marbles like eyeballs
in their pockets and ask someone
to hold their hands for small fears
of the animals left there so lifelike
and still, and I only hear laughter
coming from no identifiable source,
possibly off-camera, and I'm not being clear
about the sky which is still shaped
like your face, no, the sky is still.

NOTES

"Bright Size Life" borrows its title from the album (ECM Records, 1976) performed by Pat Metheny, Jaco Pastorius, and Bob Moses.

"Charred Beloved" borrows its title from the series of paintings by Arshile Gorky.

I would like to thank all of my friends and family in the United States for their constant support and encouragement, y muchísimas gracias a todos mis amigos y familia en Argentina por su apoyo incondicional (hay mucho de Argentina en este libro). I would also like to thank the following people for the roles they have played in helping these poems and this book come into being: Dara Wier; Lisa Russ Spaar; James Tate; David Lenson; Brian Henry; Tomaž Šalamun; John Early; all of my teachers and classmates at University of Virginia, Hollins University, and University of Massachusetts Amherst; and Gerald Costanzo, Cynthia Lamb and everyone at Carnegie Mellon University Press. Above all, gracias a Mariela y Joaquín, no hay palabras para explicar cuanto los amo.